OUT ALL DAY

OTHER BOOKS BY
JOHN DONLAN

Call Me the Breeze
(Alfred Gustav Press, 2013)

Spirit Engine
(Brick Books, 2008)

Green Man
(Ronsdale Press, 1999)

Baysville
(House of Anansi, 1993)

Domestic Economy
(Brick Books, 1990)

For Jenny
with fond best wishes

OUT ALL DAY

poems

JOHN DONLAN

RONSDALE

OUT ALL DAY
Copyright © 2018 John Donlan

RONSDALE PRESS
3350 West 21st Avenue, Vancouver, B.C., Canada V6S 1G7
www.ronsdalepress.com

Typesetting: Julie Cochrane, in New Baskerville 11 pt on 13.5
Cover Design: Julie Cochrane
Author Photo: Saskatchewan Public Library
Paper: Enviro 100 Edition, 70 lb. Husky (FSC) — 100% post-consumer
    waste, totally chlorine-free and acid-free

Ronsdale Press wishes to thank the following for their support of its publishing
program: the Canada Council for the Arts, the Government of Canada through
the Canada Book Fund, the British Columbia Arts Council, and the Province
of British Columbia through the Book Publishing Tax Credit Program.

Library and Archives Canada Cataloguing in Publication

Donlan, John, author
    Out all day: poems / John Donlan.

Issued in print and electronic formats.
ISBN 978-1-55380-547-2 (softcover)
ISBN 978-1-55380-548-9 (ebook) / ISBN 978-1-55380-549-6 (pdf)

    I. Title.

PS8557.O536O98 2018   C811'.54   C2018-904079-3   C2018-904080-7

At Ronsdale Press we are committed to protecting the environment. To this
end we are working with Canopy and printers to phase out our use of paper
produced from ancient forests. This book is one step towards that goal.

Printed in Canada by Island Blue, Victoria, B.C.

for Miriam

ACKNOWLEDGEMENTS

I am grateful to the Canada Council for the Arts, the Banff Centre for the Arts, Saskatoon Public Library, the Saskatchewan Arts Council, Massey College, and the Campbell River Museum for support during the writing of this book. Thanks also to the editors of *Canadian Literature, Event, The Antigonish Review, The Malahat Review, The Fiddlehead, Commuterlit, Dreamcatcher,* and *Grain,* where some of these poems first appeared. "At Kingfisher Creek" was a commissioned poem for the Words on the Water Writers' Festival and was featured in their program.

CONTENTS

- Shield -

– Plains –

– Cordillera –

– Elsewhere –

- Shield -

South Frontenac

South Frontenac's muggy nights in June are thick
with sex and death; on Highway 38
teenagers race the black future
beyond their cars' twin antennae of light

where frog-dotted asphalt slices the marsh
and the dark pulses with ephemerae
whose day this is to fly and mate and die;
exoskeletons tick against the glass

that curves to shield these children covertly
glancing by dash light at faces, bodies
who never again will feel so much as now
and we cooler at heart

half-remembering, dream them safe to bed.
Sunday morning in the wrecker's yard
a chipping sparrow picks bugs off the grill
of a Dodge Ram 1500 truck.

Out All Day

Finger-combing deer fly carcasses
out of what's left of my hair
I puzzle over my most minute machinery,
the "cascade of chemical reactions,"

proteins, electric snakes bunched,
their branched and folded chains
like overtwisted flex cord, flickering
with life, without thought, without intention.

The path from there to here
has too many connections, overwhelms,
as when a widower, hearing his wife's name,
weeps.

Dragonflies hover and dart like gunships
and I scratch my head, and the pond's
lacy scrim of lily pads might map the molecule
of happiness, thirty thousand atoms long.

The Idiocy of Rural Life

Coming out of a funk
guilt and despair stream off like smoke
from a burning CN locomotive
near here, June night, deep bush, mosquito hell.

What melting, boiling, slow
collision, rain, erosion, debris flow
(half rock, half water) this Shield was,
now cool, lichened elephant-colour.

Soon we're back to atoms, no nature,
never mind. Chameleon lovers,
gifted as mirrors, we ache to belong
yet stay out all night

staring at moonlight. I have time to burn,
to list tools your son can use
to be a man: Robertson screwdriver,
Mastercraft hammer, lifetime guarantee.

I Am

love song, something about a fool
and tears; the vole's chief keener as he flies
(it's all our deaths) in the hawk's claws; two white
eggs the anxious whippoorwill abandoned.

In the sight of at least four hundred trees
promise practising kindness more often,
not disdain her pleasure, purchases
no matter the coal-fired factories in China:

what is that your business? How many trees
do you kill with your stupid poetry?
You envy her happiness.

Wind ruffles the pond surface sky blue,
calming to forest green, grey, yellow, overlain
on the bottom's bright carbon-sink brown.

Storm

The breeze slows, the pond mirrors
a bruise-blue cloudwall rising.
Hailstones batter the forest
and strew the water with tattered green.

The poet's I
slips from its tedious spinning
into the seethe; molecules of sap
breathe from broken vessels of leaves.

Not every creature can take shelter:
insects, even small birds
will be feasts for scavengers
as the white windrows melt

under the following sun.
A snapping turtle dozes on a beaver lodge,
head sagged on long neck like a dead thing.
Inside, beaver kits croon for food.

Lotus

Today I spent too long breathing the scent
the wind carried across the water:
acres of white water lilies, thousands.
At the far shore

under the forest wall, they're dots;
here, they could be emblems
of enlightenment and perfect peace.
Disordered by their perfume,

I imagine this afternoon unending,
I jump the job, never to return,
while my colleagues drudge
and laugh that I call this work.

That's how far I am from enlightenment
and perfect peace. When I look out again
the lilies have closed against the sun,
fisted in green casings until tomorrow.

Days

Fall blows in: drying leaves
clatter and flash pale undersides.
A mink frog yips and skitters over the water:
a life in four summers.

This map, my skin
is speckled, wrinkled, scarred; what was this life?
"*Diem perdidi*," Emperor Titus said:
"I've lost a day" — one without a good deed.

His legions had other marching orders:
level Jerusalem. *First, do no harm*;
impossible for any animal, yet not to try — Hear that?
Some creature, unseen, nearby, a clear

clink, clink, like a key on stone
makes its nature known
to give and find pleasure,
make something of the day.

Mink

for Philip Larkin

A mink, jittery, neckless, serpentine,
ransacks the shore three times an hour.
A flash, frog-belly white — devoured.
"Your blood is yours, your blood is mine."

Mucky scurf, planetary skin
born of accident, rock and air and light,
we feed each other and delight
in the wet machine that makes us kin,

builds molecules as a child makes
a flower of wooden blocks,
gives every life the means to read and talk
World. Being here is all it takes

to fill tick-full with the beauty on view
till love alone drives my heart
yet still admire your killing art;
I'm with you.

Four Otters

Four otters forage together
the length of Lily Pond, spines pouring under
then heads-up, jaws shearing and crushing
frogs, minnows, pollywogs, crayfish,

diving again.
They call to each other
as I watch them out of sight in a blur of flowers.
I think of them crossing the lane

for the next pond, the neighbour's land,
past "Live Bait" signs and "Standing Timber Wanted"
— but that's too far: I've imagined them
into a zone of harm where next winter

they'll drown under the ice in beaver traps.
Look, here they come back.
They make two more passes.
Nebulas of algae breathe for us.

Strong as Life

Two ants tow half a caterpillar,
pulling against each other, dropping
the load, stick legs, bodies
unstopping, epic.

Though your bones break every time you're moved
in your hospital bed, your body lives.
Grandmother and her hydrocephalic
son died after thirty hours of labour;

the contractions stopped when blood
loss and exhaustion killed her with the child.
Near the stream, a young red-shouldered hawk
screams and screams, *kee-ah*. Another

flies toward it carrying a frog. If
imagination was as strong as life
I'd be that frog, I'd look down and say,
"I'm flying, I've turned into a bird."

Earthquake

A groan, far off —
"Did you feel it? *I* felt and heard; downstairs
she noticed nothing." North of Ottawa
two plates of the earth's skull scraped past each other.

Toronto shook; in Quebec, a church
cracked. Rock-solid world
trips you panicked and woozy
surfing lava currents miles down.

Yet how good a world: up in the air
as if to shelter you the trees breathe out
water for white cloud as they eat the sun.
Everywhere you are kindly reminded

of death and return, not to be grim
or broody about it but to remember
not to waste time and to have serious fun
like otters ice-sliding when winter comes.

Whirligig

End of July, trees call it a season
shut down their green workshops and let them rust.
Bumper cars in water dimples, whirligig
beetles zoom and carom, rippling moonlight.

Perseids sing their fire songs
as they streak our black stadium, burning up
into atoms of atmosphere.
Crickets begin, and a thousand insect voices

(scraping legs are a voice), and deer mice trill
high urgent love calls from the trees.
On an outflung arm of the Milky Way
we wonder what to do and what to say

from our lush life, so postmodern, so free
to equal their conviction, their necessity.
Long past moonset we lie outside and listen
and stare up into the star-hazy night.

Waiting

The pond has dropped a foot over the summer;
you couldn't pole a punt across it now.
New-risen loamy flats and yellowing lilies'
braided roots, thick as a leg, are drying

in fierce September sun; dark trunks of trees
that drowned and fell and sank
after beaver dammed the trickling creek
turn pale as dust.

Radiant storms of words
and images criss-crossing air and settling
in devices electron-thin can't reach
into valleys tucked under rocky ridges

of the Shield. Hours here
dissolve the city's crust of irritants
and distractions: your ambition's focussed
as a frog's, waiting for the bright fly.

Property

Little frogs, little frogs, Ontario bourgeois
each on your bit of shoreline
you dive in sequence as I pass
as if it all were mine,

the pond, the rocks, the trees,
the clouds, the sun.
You don't know the panic of property,
the folded sheets, the bank account, the loaded gun.

Ignore the highway howling upwind.
Yellow and orange leaves fall to the water
and clusters of white-pine needles double-twinned
smooth a rusty coverlet over the daughter

shore's bare shoulders where the clear-cut fell.
The logger's boy has a grandchild in town
six years old today; the pines are sixty feet tall
and no one will ever cut them down.

By Charm, By Stealth

What do the trees roar
into the wind, their crowns
threshing, fervent as fans?
"Despair, despair?"

No, that's a different voice,
disturbingly near
intimate warm and clear.
Given the choice

you'd never hear it at all
but you keep your friends close
and your enemies closer.
The tree frog's gargling, twittery call

is penetrating, full of itself.
All the frogs listening know
just what their chances are and go
on calling, by charm, by stealth.

North of Seven

Roads up here
"north of the IQ line"
follow the curve of the land
like a strap over a woman's shoulder.

Downslope
weedy streams invite you
to paddle off into prehistory.
Ompah, a short portage

between English and Algonquin.

Clouds, sacs of water like ourselves,
symbols of soul's high desire
show how the wind blows

over the sawmill at Vennachar
taking the tall trees into its mouth
for all of us.

For the Baysville Public School Reunion

My old two-room schoolhouse is gone
(grades one to four downstairs, a lady teacher;
upstairs the last four grades, a man)
and the brash new brick one closed in sixty-six.

How high the hip roof loomed! Yet we would throw
hex nuts with string streamers back and forth
over it, and those red-white-and-blue foam-rubber balls.
Here, gone. To vanish, and return.

Most of my class of eight survive
though shy, lovely Nellie Lunnen's dead,
suffering and brave under her mother's hand-me-down
Mother Hubbards, who captured my hand

for our class photo. Proud, diffident,
beaten, defiant, secret, our frozen faces
can never age or die; they snatch us back
out of time each time they catch our eye.

Not Screaming

In cool September wind
leaves tug against branches
wanting to let go, become soil.
A bee fumbles pale violet asters, a

russet and scarlet dragonfly
soaks sun off a page — few
insects remain: most birds have left
for the south, left

silence to fill with leaf sound
or ravens' sepulchral mutterings.
Someone sometimes too much in the moment, chilly,
invisible from space on the blue spinning globe

indulges in a warm bath of regret
at summer ending; thus wanders
from the Way Things Are; briefly awakes
not screaming, spinning at one thousand miles an hour.

Testament

This "over-mature" poplar
broader than me at breast height,
soon will topple, turn to forest floor.
From seven storeys up a porcupine

has strewn a ring of chopped branchlets
around the base, their tender twigs snibbed off.
Tonight the porcupine could feast; or a fisher
dodging the murderous tail, could tear

its face till, pouring blood, it faints and dies.
I'll have it easy, my death
undramatic, my body
at some expense tidied away.

Or to make an end by this beaver pond:
no food, no drink: in a few days I'd be gone.
The fisher could eat what flesh there was
and the porcupine gnaw the bones for calcium.

The George River Caribou Herd

Along Devonshire a line of dump trucks idles;
as one crawls roaring out of its square pit
like an angry mastodon
another creeps downslope to be loaded

with blue-grey glacier dregs the city digs and builds on.
Bloor Street westbound is pale with their dust;
traffic twirls it high, the wind snatches it
up and around the world. Some even falls

on the George River caribou herd
walking from James Bay to the Labrador Sea
800,000 strong. If you were there
the dust would be blackflies. You'd hear only

ankles clicking, the blurts and murmurs of caribou bellies,
the rasp of teeth and lips tearing the lichen free,
the soft knock of their hooves on stone,
the light breeze blowing around the world.

Looking North from the Thirteenth Floor of the Robarts Library

This fresh-washed atmosphere's
a plane's busy hiss, as if
we'll soon lift off
above clouds trudging west

to Mississauga.
Tonight's frost will signal the turn
of Toronto's green roof below
to red, orange, yellow, skeleton.

In the elevator I inhale
beauty and youth as we ascend
into time's mercies. We can't hear
Hurricane Sandy sob and falter on the walls,

hunger wail through plastic-sheeted camps,
bullets splatter against the school bus,
sirens.
      The terror is absorbed into the books,
infinitesimal in their great heart.

Immanent

Slower than snow
aspen seed-fluffs'
million perfect parachutes

fall, fur the bay.
Swirls of slut's wool; what's
the point of them?

Bodying hope
in such near-nothingness
doom with so little gravity

they carry us
a moment in trust
down the slope of air.

Caducity

After the clear-cut's catastrophe
rising forest life welcomes the dead:
leaves and twigs that fail are gnawed to mulch
by insect jaws, digested by microbes;

a branchless snag becomes a totem
condo, cave mouths each with its family;
when finally it falls its tons of mass
are soon more living matter than dead wood.

Death builds the hungry soil which feeds us all.
A philosopher says this is happiness,
this failing and falling, this rising up.
An impersonal kind of happiness.

I don't like fishing now: I only went this year
to be with my oldest friend. We towed home six
smallmouth, fresh and alive, tethered through
rasp jaw and gaping scarlet gill.

One by one I clubbed them dead and Gary cleaned.
One had somehow swum free but still it stayed
beside the rest, slow, weary, nuzzling.
I don't know what it was: it looked like love.

Mole

I'm here all year;
under a rough leaf jacket
in cool carbon clutter
(where the rot sets in)

I dig, I hunt,
I lust, I doze.
The world is mineral particles, and mould,
gritty grey or iron-orange or black

(but down here everything is black).
Satan-like, I go to and fro in the earth
and admit to neither good nor evil.
My prey is in the upper layer:

I listen to a worm hitch itself near
and the scrape, scrape of a cricket's casing.
When tunnel roofs collapse I flee the light,
star-nosed, innocent.

White Clover

They line back-country roads like crowds
swaying as interesting persons pass,
parting for driveways into forest-walled yards
where weekenders or lifers stare —

Now, who might *you* be?
— and we stare back.
To Township trucks we raise two fingers from the wheel,
the faces in the cabs almost unseen;

here as with any steady kind regard
met and held, we nod. This grave
bow, this slow lowering of the head
says more than any wave (that false

dismissive distancing gesture); salutes
losses survived, lonelinesses, our private
common core; illuminates the root
of love itself: I see you, I accept.

Two Foot

Why does this place flow and flow
through the mind? Like a neglected child
rocking itself to sleep to summon pleasure
you make its loveliness appear and pass.

The south branch of the Muskoka River
drops in a black sheet over Two Foot
granite sill across the channel
level as a table.
Tea-tinted foam heads quiver on the gravel bar.
Timeless river, immediate in memory
wilderness between two dams.

grabbed a branch over the rapids
current dragging at the sunk canoe
legs caught under a thwart
finally kicked free

arse over teakettle down the rapids
saved the tackle-box with the mickey

In a slow pool
you swim naked
long-haired pale water nymphs
cajole fur traders, explorers
to berth their canoes, safe in the soft moss
take off their shirts, slip into myth.

You hike back down the bush trail
blood humming river music.

Bark

A bark
in the woods.
Another.
Coyotes, or wolves.

Back.
The pond's still here
but I've
been running deer.

- Plains -

Almighty Voice

The book that tells us how to be
lies always open: yellow elm leaves sweep
past in prairie breeze, prairie dust
that's everywhere in Saskatoon. Our pride

is our killing winters: survival
chills us country-calm
country-cooperative
even to strangers; almost innocent.

Talk of the harvest everywhere: delay,
grain "lodged" — flattened — in wind and rain.
Almighty Voice, starving, eating poplar bark
silenced 1897 age twenty-two

still tells us the land
doesn't care who she teaches.
Two peregrines hunt the river park.
A Sulfur, battered pale, struggles upwind.

Wanuskewin

Grazing herds so vast
they took a man three days to ride through.
From a rise you could see buffalo every way
brown to the round horizon.

Earth's gifts remain: sun, rain,
the clear air that flows on forever
through blue grama grass and wolf willow
over the cliff edge, the empty river.

November, Saskatoon, Saskatchewan

The city with the most Canadian sky.
Under what looks like tons of Rogers brown sugar
Co-op Boulevard is streaked and marbled with ice
the grey of October lakes reflecting snow clouds.

The sun is blazing but nothing is melting.
A little colder, and rock salt won't melt it
(potash, pale-salmon buried prairie oceans)
and skates won't work, like skating on brick.

How does this most Canadian of skies —
not yesterday's, steam-coloured, flat as paint,
leaking icy dust —
but tomorrow's bottomless blue

bless, drench the view from Cranberry Flats
west across the river to the vanishing point,
untroubled by trees or mountains, nothing
bigger than a barn — in light, in love?

Fine Day

Jean Beliveau died this week, city hall flags
half-mast. Could he ever deke! (Our sure
anticipation of joy when he played.)

Ice fog hoars the spruces; each bare elm
twig's white-crystal-furred, whose flimsy castles
shatter at a gust, shrug, topple in

on themselves and fall like clumsy snowflakes
into the steaming, still-unfrozen river
clotting with slush, northbound for Hudson Bay.

On Broadway Bridge I lean over the rail,
the concrete pier a prow cracking white plates.
Open water; thirty below: SaskPower
ate its coal mountain, still fevers the river.

Poundmaker

As I walked home one winter night
a white hare stood in Temperance Street.
Its black-tipped ears and backward-looking eye
attended my approach.

You're not from here, it said.

Spirit of the place, when we are gone,
our homes and cars and streets returned
to prairie, you will remain,
sniffing for swelling buds above the snow.

To make peace
with grief that rends me
I remember that winter night,
the great white hare.

- Cordillera -

City Birds

They spit sunflower seeds and scratch the black
wet-all-winter earth, darkly watched
by glaring cats; if they're stabbed with fears
and sorrows of a short fragile life

they never let on but gamely flit and peck,
flirt and court, their pea-sized hearts
thrumming with lust and hunger: now. Now.
Street lights on at three: we're in the egg,

the very yolk of winter's solstice,
eating darkness while light pecks our shell,
still not ground down or blunted horribly
despite the shocking mirror;

no, Christ's death, we're
seven again, expecting a mystery
rabbit, Easter chocolate,
sweet white and yellow centres.

Shadetree Mechanic

You can read the Rockies like a book;
lifting their heavy pages
you help them crumble, fossil letters fracturing at a look.
You learn the craft of ages,

reinventing from what's broken,
bricoleur of nature's conspicuous waste;
walk the mountain path, hurry erosion,
heartsick at our disgrace.

Yet the hard grind
against mineral heights seeps down, it feeds,
swells sweet valley bottoms.
       Mind
you don't claim more than you need

of guilt, a kind of power:
you're not so important:
just one living
witness of the hour.

At Kingfisher Creek

Silt-slimed, ash-grey
salmon corpses strewn like cordwood
clog Kingfisher Creek. After high water
some droop from branches like Dali watches.

Carried far by bears and eagles, some say,
minerals in their bones feed the forest:
but this scene is best explained
by the constant voice-over of water on stone

which tells us nothing
yet somehow changes our minds for the better.
The last voice exhausted salmon hear
sings through the long slow winter sleep

of eggs clinging to sand against the pull
of summer, of downhill, of ocean future.

Weed Trees

Weed trees block the view.
Ocean and mountain

can't see us
and don't care if they do.

They're far too busy
making the air

making a home for the world
to live in — the hardworking

chickadee, the idling
poet sitting and staring

beyond death.

Without hope,

without despair,
a sunset black armada of

crows commute home
from sweet muscled jelly

torn from broken shells.
The tide rises.

Bivalves breathe relief
in saltwater sighs.

- Elsewhere -

Port of Vancouver

between railroad ties

green fur of tender shoots

Saskatchewan wheat

Spring

spring

tractor drags

gull clouds

Storm

rain puddle

still

storm-cloud-coloured

Cherry Blossoms

cherry petals

swirl in pink drifts

on some lucky streets

Junco

junco

belly full of lichen

still foraging

Dance

no breeze

fall evening

gnats' last dance

Hiss

over the hiss

of sleet-static

bird talk

Twig

twig

scratches on snow

wind's no-name

Wandering Spirit

in memoriam Elise Partridge, 1958–2015

When the heart, that shy, wise animal
comfortable in its failing cage

wakes in pain
pounding tenderly for attention

we offer only this comfort: we breathe
swell red ribs hanging off hatrack spine,
flex cartilage invisibly gleaming

so that our sad lieutenant has full room
to pulse sorrow and rage to every cell,
feed this body the unfeeling world.

Thank You, Grief

Grief, I'm tired of your visit today
shuffling your faded photographs of the dead
who will never hear my apologies;
your private viewings of women I loved

and lost, somehow;
even my cats and dogs, their tiny bones
mouldering in old towels and blankets under back gardens
across Canada —

Grief, this is too much!
You're hiding something. This pain near my heart
pierces my shoulder blade: it hurts to move,
to live. Each injury

heals slower than the last.
Thank you, Grief: you've reminded me of my death
and that I prefer the lost past to the lost future
and when this little pain ends so will you.

Philosophers

We're two healthy animals still
at sixty-five and fifty-three;
your daughter's death
and all our losses haven't been able to kill
even that too-often-early-defeated tendril of spirit, glee;

bushwhacking in to the pond with a couple of beers
like kids sneaking out of alien rules
to someplace beautiful where mere survival is the only clear
necessity, with time left over, we'd be fools

if we didn't realize the very air
we were breathing in was making us better, more
like everything there;
the whore

devouring beak in all we lovely saw
all-connected as it thrives and kills and dies
quickened the moment; raw
flesh we are, with every bird that flies.

Religion

What must it be like, to lie on the pond
bottom, muck soft under your back,
pale stalks rising all around in the gloom
while you drown?

Drowning is painless, survivors say,
unfrightening, a strangely serene surrender
to memory, and nothing — And after?
Most people believe

some best part of us will always live:
comforting, but unlikely.
The late sun is glittering off the leaves;
their *hush, hush* is infinitely soothing.

Seeing and hearing are the best parts of being here:
they're how the world's constancy and love
enter us, convince us this life
is all, and comfort enough.

Here, There

Wind drifts the craft.
White pines do the hula —
hello, suggestively waving their limbs,
whale grace, majesty. My ruined plumage

stirs, salutes, forgives
an old man's being old, inevitable failure.
When I become the rain, will you forgive
my wetting your hair, wetting your face,

running the ink in your new poem? Because
when you're all over, you're all over.
Mainly cloudy, with a mix of sun and cloud
later today, when the poem will take place.

Call me the breeze;
when you hear J.J. Cale's rock-steady beat
get up and dance for all of us who know
where music comes from and where it goes.

Portrait

In the thirties, single, poor (some days
she couldn't afford the nickel carfare
for a trolley to her sister across town)
she paid for her portrait in ink and coloured wash:
pensive, determined (she owned Shaw's
Intelligent Woman's Guide to Socialism).
Her mother kept the girls out of the kitchen
and dying said, "Look after your father and brothers."
The mad angry grandfather in the back room
died in legal custody. She remembers gold
floating on air, shimmering sheets of foil
for her father's sign-painting: *Salada,*
Black Cat, Empire Hotel.
On holiday from Riverdale Isolation Hospital
for friendship and protection she bought a dog,
to hitchhike Cape Breton on her holidays.
A portrait is a life without a story.

Oxygen

Shrunk like a nut in your comfortable chair
you are still not safe; killer
oxygen is ripping limbs
off the holy family of your DNA,

unravelling you faster than you can mend.
No more than a growing tree
can you choose to stand apart
from the dark networks that feed your roots

or the sweet water rising in you.
You reflect sunlight and show yourself
even as you slyly palm and eat
its magic bead.

Which part of your porous brain
is in truth you alone? Right now you are
only the pond, its shores and contents
and the wind too soft to make a sound.

Jan van Eyck's "The Madonna of Chancellor Rolin"

In this picture paradise is paved.
The floor of Mary's room is tiled
in stars of marble. Columns all around
enclose some heavenly receiving room.

An angel hovers, holding Mary's crown,
each jewel real. Solemn, fat as a berry
Child Christ blesses the doubting Chancellor's gaze
on his mother's lap.

Frozen in ritual piety
the Chancellor wishes he was someplace else
but he paid to be in this picture, and by God,
he'll get his money's worth.

It's a forbidding scene. No one looks happy
or directly at anyone else.
The baby has bags under his eyes, his mother
holds him at arm's length like a bomb.

Mies van der Rohe said God is in the details.
Here van Eyck so packs every brushed inch
that even a Chancellor smells mystery.
Outside this scene of stony grace, a landscape,

a fashionable picture in a picture:
past farms with cattle diminutive as beetles
and men and women tiny with perspective
a river winds towards us from the hills
widens into the spired city surrounding
and disappears below the garden wall
where level with medieval steepletops
red-turbaned Jan van Eyck and Hubert peer

over a carved stone balcony at Earth
perfect below, the book of happiness
open to distant eyes.
Looks like they're laughing.

Sestina: Facts of History

I'm new here. From my chaste bed, a naked
foam slab on the floor of an apartment house
in Ottawa, I trace ice crystals on the window.
Nearby Bank Street buses drum the frozen
brick-hard city, heavy with bodies
of civil servants. A loose pane rattles.

My wife will join me in a month. Unrattled
by solitude, I read *China Men*; foreign bodies
slaved here twenty wifeless years, half naked,
rock-drilling, the tunnel's end a shrinking window.
Some died of Gold Mountain's cold heart, frozen
with loss, face to the wall of a bunkhouse.

A week before work starts, I house
an alien — Asian flu. My teeth rattle
against a water glass as fever burns the body
clean of regret. At last, hungry and naked,
I prowl as weak light whitens the window.
A sparrow cheeps at thirty below, unfrozen.

My month alone, that little past, is shucked off, frozen
in memory like the skin a snake, naked
and newly bright, abandons. The parched husk rattles
in papery imitation of a body
as I touch the delicate-scaled tubular window
on absence, shiver at the stir of slither's empty house.

The facts of history show humankind naked
as animals, until we dressed our past with a body
of pictures and stories. That empty apartment, that house
we soon moved to, all those windows
open on a better life — they're frozen
in snapshots we posed for; click, then a rattle

of laughter, relief at capturing another prize for the body
of images we've built ourselves. But the house
of cards and letters memory lives in slips, slides rattle
in the projector, clatter back to the box, frozen
in plastic almost forever — improbable windows
on a manufactured past. The naked

truth frozen in every instant rattles
like hail on our bodies, we open attention's window,
the icy facts melt in our naked hands, in the mind's house.

The Muscle Motor Molecule Myosin

Smaller than the wavelength of light
like a drunk walking
a length of pipe, myosin staggers battered
by jet-fast random atoms

each raised leg flung into all possible
positions, like Monty Python's
Ministry of Silly Walks
in chaos-driven steps

until one fits and locks;
work gets done;
heat-maddened water spins CANDUs;
I stumble into poetry;

house finches sing
delirious with lust without a plan
feathered heads are turned and hearts
are lifted and again it's spring.

To My Heart

Heart, you're wearing out;
your two grey scars still flex and close
like a hand around a working tool
every evening readier for rest.

For all your hard wear you are
more tender than ever;
the woman you love
grows ever dearer, the least

creature thrives on your benign
neglect, and you're forgiven
the days you work in darkness
and feel nothing at all.

The Master

for John Fraser

What has happened to Robertson Davies?
He has become his darkening bronze statue,
his nose affectionately rubbed and shining;
he has become an eleventh-century monastery

in downtown Toronto, where monks play pranks
and study, study, study, study and teach
love of learning; he has become the hall
where Engineer debates Philosopher,

the Common Room where the best students greet
the neighbourhood's struggling children
and help them with their homework; he has become
the scholar who feeds the squirrel who teases the dog

who sometimes will come when her master whistles,
who is the Master Dogwalker, the guiding
hand and spirit and Master of Massey College
who is, and more, what has happened to Robertson Davies.

Cat's Paw

You clung to absence,
traced the rounded lips
of loss on the worn heels

of your father's second-best high-cuts:
until the weekend they were all
you had of him to love.

Now absence
claims you, blurs and fades
memory's blueprints, unravels

old shared stories: remember?
No. Only
that rising falling curve

back of each heel
once printed "Cat's Paw"
factory-fresh.

Sorrow

Sorrow and I have been avoiding
each other lately: I refuse to wallow
especially after what — let's face it — has
been a lucky life: I never thought

I'd make thirty, coming from where
I come from. And I'm sick, frankly, of sorrow's
weight, its drag, its melodrama, Marley's
ghost howling its hell of lost chances.

On the occasions when we were together
sorrow, like a nurse, like a narcotic
slowed the world, fuzzed out
pain and confusion while I healed myself.

Maybe I clung to it too long
but it was familiar
and a comfort, like imagining
I can master sorrow, or its reasons.

Angels of Order

Age aches and stabs, the stars
whirl in their courses, flying ever faster
from each other since
ever so long ago. There's comfort

in a story: chaos and pain
have no dominion, wounds are healed.
Angels of order are everywhere

bright angels nuzzling us
avidly gobbling, licking our
sad dust into immortality.

Our granddaughters are dreamy,
happy in their cloud of friends.
When will they last
remember us?

Grackle

in memoriam Steve Saunders, 1957–2015

Something's not right. Late summer,
still screaming at the parent to be fed?
This chick's soon going back to nature's
earthy churn, like Geoffrey's jettisoned

straw hat — or you, transubstantiated
into gas, scraps of bone and ash
scattered on your favourite island.
Always fully, fiercely in your body, you'd swim there

every summer, almost out of sight
below the dark-treed shore. You won't come back.
You live on in us as an ache, a lack,
an urge to straighten certain defeated postures,

neck back, head high: after the funeral
I thought a hawk spiraling up was you.

Field

Free of work, routine, someplace to be
soul can swell, balloon-like, empty
even of itself, an eye
reporting to no one
as if there were no earth, no sky,
no sun. This is the soul's
work, desolate moment
in Perth Home Hardware parking lot
as asphalt cracks above the buried
field shouldering up into the light.

Paroxetine

In his eighth decade
he reeks again of adolescent angst
yet feels little more than a frozen sea;
his chemical new friend
is fiddling with his funk — to call back pleasure,
absent since last year's fifth funeral
which seemed excessive.
"If you're lucky you'll bury all your friends."

At the wake, an old wife, an old lover,
one pretending not to know the other.
Angry at strangers:
they're alive when his friend is dead.
No desire
except for sleep,
sleep.
Coming around, remembering
Leonard Cohen: "Survival is success."

Sestina: Why I Say Sorry So Often

I don't know why
this is even a thing. It's muscular kindness. I
admit we seem cool northern characters, but say
we're in Loblaws and we almost touch. Sorry
acknowledges our right to ignore each other: so
it's also its opposite: often

we're happy the bubble's broken. That's why
these little transgressions are so charged: I
expect they more often lead to marriage than, say,
a bar chat might. Sorry
is also how I feel about Claudus Stroud, so
blond and beautiful you could weep. Often

I'd see him crutching his tiny waist and legs along. Why
sorry? I
suppose empathy is just to say
I imagine being Claudus, dragging those sorry
polio-stricken leg-ironed legs so
far every day. (Though often

he was in the company of the nicest girls.) Why
is kindness our shy, secret strength? I
think evolution has its say
in why we help each other. Sorry
to get so
explainy-preachy: often

I give our lives more why
than they need. I
suppose it's comforting. Say
you love me. Sorry
to ask, but I so
need to hear it, and often.

No need to ask why:
you know as well as I
do that survival can depend on hearing someone say
they love you and that they're the opposite of sorry
you're in the world. So
I'll say it too, early and often.

Saying it isn't just a Canadian
cultural tic; we know sorry's grounded in love
so that's why I say it so often.

Tooth and Claw

They cut you open and drink your blood
but they're drops and you're the flood.
If only they didn't sting!
And itch! The spring
snuffled and drowned and now it's fall.
We don't understand it at all.
A sense of impending doom
tries to fill the room
but you're getting too big for your britches.
You alone will be dead. The sons of bitches
will drink blood as long as there's water in ditches.

Chuck Berry

The great American artist
who invented the word "motorvatin'"
injected homemade slave songs, sad old blues
with the energy and speed of Detroit machines

and the Detroit iron they made: magic carpets
that float you like a raja over the land
as when in dreams we fly upright, powered
by the slightest pressure of a few toes.

After supper, doing our homework
we could get Double-You-Bee-Zee from Boston
on our tiny transistor radios:
the Hollywood Flames, Little Richard, the Coasters —

in my snowbound northern ignorance
I didn't even know they were black.
But they were brown-skinned handsome men
singing us into a new kind of freedom.

NOTES

"Days," line 9: Titus ordered the destruction of Jerusalem, 70 C.E.

"The Idiocy of Rural Life." The phrase is Marx's.

"North of Seven." Ompah, an Algonquin word meaning "short portage," is a village in North Frontenac Township, 100 km southwest of Ottawa. The portage is between the Mississippi and Madawaska River systems.

Kapapamahchakwew (Wandering Spirit), 1845–1885, was a Cree war chief with Big Bear's band. After the massacre of nine settlers at Frog Lake, he and seven others were hanged in the largest mass execution in Canadian history. On the scaffold, Wandering Spirit sang a love song to his wife.

Kamiokisihkwew (Fine Day), 1852–1935, was a Cree war chief and shaman of the River People band. He participated in the Northwest Resistance of 1885. After the imposition of Treaty Six he led his people in the difficult transition from buffalo hunting to farming.

Pîhtokahanapiwiyin (Poundmaker), 1842–1886, was a Cree chief who during a famine plundered a deserted trading post for rations. He subsequently led the last battle of the Northwest Resistance in which the settler militia was defeated. After seven months in prison, broken in spirit and health, he died three weeks after his release.

Kitchimanitowaya (Almighty Voice), 1875–1897, was arrested in 1895 for slaughtering a cow. He escaped from jail and remained a fugitive until 1897 when, after inflicting seven vigilante casualties, he and two young relatives were murdered in an artillery barrage. As his One Arrow reserve members watched his final battle, his mother sang his death song.

COMPANION READING

Alberts, Bruce, et al. *Molecular Biology of the Cell.* 5th edition. New York: Garland Science, 2008.

Bray, Dennis. *Wetware: A Computer in Every Living Cell.* New Haven: Yale University Press, 2009.

Goodsell, David S. *Our Molecular Nature: The Body's Motors, Machines, and Messages.* New York: Copernicus, 1996.

Harold, Franklin M. *The Way of the Cell: Molecules, Organisms and the Order of Life.* New York: Oxford University Press, 2001.

Hengeveld, R. "Two Approaches to the Study of the Origin of Life." *Acta Biotheoretica,* v. 55, 2007, pp. 97–131.

Hengeveld, R., and M.A. Fedonkin. "Bootstrapping the Energy Flow in the Beginning of Life." *Acta Biotheoretica,* v. 55, 2007, pp. 181–226.

Hoffmann, Peter M. *Life's Ratchet: How Molecular Machines Extract Order from Chaos.* New York: Basic Books, 2012.

Hunter, Lawrence E. *The Processes of Life: An Introduction to Molecular Biology.* Cambridge, Mass.: MIT Press, 2009.

Loewenstein, R. Werner. *The Touchstone of Life: Molecular Information, Cell Communication, and the Foundations of Life.* New York: Oxford University Press, 1999.

Lovelock, James. *The Ages of Gaia: A Biography of Our Living Earth.* New York: Norton, 1988.

Luoma, Jon R. *The Hidden Forest: The Biography of an Ecosystem.* New York: Henry Holt, 1999.

Margulis, Lynn, and Dorion Sagan. *Microcosmos: Four Billion Years of Evolution from Our Microbial Ancestors.* Berkeley: University of California Press, 1997.

Margulis, Lynn, and Dorion Sagan. *What Is Life?* New York: Simon and Schuster, 1995.

Radison, Garry. *Fine Day: Plains Cree Warrior, Shaman, and Elder.* Yorkton, Smoke Ridge Books, 2013.

Radison, Garry. *Kapepamahchekwew, Wandering Spirit: Plains Cree War Chief.* Yorkton, Smoke Ridge Books, 2009.

Rensberger, Boyce. *Life Itself: Exploring the Realm of the Living Cell.* New York, Oxford University Press, 1996.

Schneider, Eric D., and Dorion Sagan. *Into the Cool: Energy Flow, Thermodynamics, and Life.* Chicago: University of Chicago Press, 2005.

Schrödinger, Erwin. *What Is Life?* with *Mind and Matter* and *Autobiographical Sketches.* Cambridge: Cambridge University Press, 1992.

Volk, Tyler. *Gaia's Body: Toward a Physiology of Earth.* Cambridge: MIT Press, 2003.

Williams, R.J.P., and J.J.R. Fraústo da Silva. *The Chemistry of Evolution: The Development of Our Ecosystem.* New York: Elsevier, 2005.

Wolpert, Lewis. *How We Live and Why We Die: The Secret Lives of Cells.* London: Faber, 2009.

Zimmer, Karl. *Microcosm: E. Coli and the New Science of Life.* New York: Pantheon Books, 2008.

ABOUT THE AUTHOR

John Donlan is the author of five previous collections of poetry: *Domestic Economy* (Brick Books, 1990, reprinted 2008), *Baysville* (Anansi, 1993, 2003), *Green Man* (Ronsdale, 1999, 2014), *Spirit Engine* (Brick, 2008, 2014), and *Call Me the Breeze* (Alfred Gustav Press, 2013). He is also the author of *A Guide to Research at Your Library* (Ontario Library Association, 2002). He is an editor with Brick Books, and was the 2012–2013 Barbara Moon Editorial Fellow at Massey College, University of Toronto, the 2014–2015 Writer in Residence at Saskatoon Public Library, and the 2016–2017 Haig-Brown Writer in Residence in Campbell River. He divides his time between Vancouver, B.C., and South Frontenac, Ontario. Visit John's website at www.johndonlan.wordpress.com.